Lights
of the Louvre

This book was published for Electricité de France on the occasion
of the lighting of the Louvre courtyards.

Designed and published by
Les éditions Textuel,
7, rue Lacuée, 75004 Paris.
Editor
Maria Félix Frazao
Contributors
Henri Alekan, Geneviève
Bresc, Arlette Farge,
Guy Nicot
Assistant Editors
Nathalie Bourgeois, Marie
Desplechin, Brigitte Morin
Art Director
Luce Pénot
Planning
Annouchka Walther
Design
Caroline Keppy,
Sandrine Roux
Translated by
Glenn Naumovitz

© EDF, 1995.
Communication
Department,
2, rue Louis Murat,
75384 Paris Cedex 08

ISBN : 2-909317-12-9
Copyright: May 1995

20   Combining Stone and Light

      by Guy Nicot

32   From Chinese Lanterns to Everyday Lighting

      by Geneviève Bresc

44   In the Sheltering Shadow of Paris

      by Arlette Farge

56   Changing Light is Changing Life

      by Henri Alekan

I to XVI   Lighting the Louvre: An Inside Account

Preface

The Louvre Museum has the historical good fortune of being located not in a faceless, functional building, but in a palace where French kings lived for centuries. They and their successors asked the architects to take special care in designing the facades.

The Louvre Museum has an obligation to preserve and show this architectural heritage off to its best advantage. The Etablissement du Grand Louvre and the palace's chief architect, Mr. Guy Nicot, a member of the Institut de France, have accomplished an oustanding achievement that merits high acclaim.

Electricité de France has helped us pursue another goal: making the Louvre more accessible and encouraging pass-ersby to visit the palace in the hopes that one day they will enter the museum itself. Lighting the cour Carrée and cour Napoléon facades, a project my predecessor, Michel Laclotte, followed very closely, goes a long way towards achieving this aim. Paris night owls are once again coming to the Louvre out of curiosity and admiration.

They are curious because light attracts and signals life and movement. The museum is bustling with activity after dark. Exhibitions, concerts, films, readings and lectures take place in the evening. The bookstore, cafés and restaurants are open late and on Mondays and Wednesdays the collections can be visited until ten p.m.

They are filled with admiration because Electricité de France and the museum's directors agreed on a project that respects and enhances the architecture rather than treats it like a spectacular stage set.

We would like to thank Electricité de France for the fine job they have done as well as for this book.

Pierre Rosenberg
President and director of the Louvre Museum

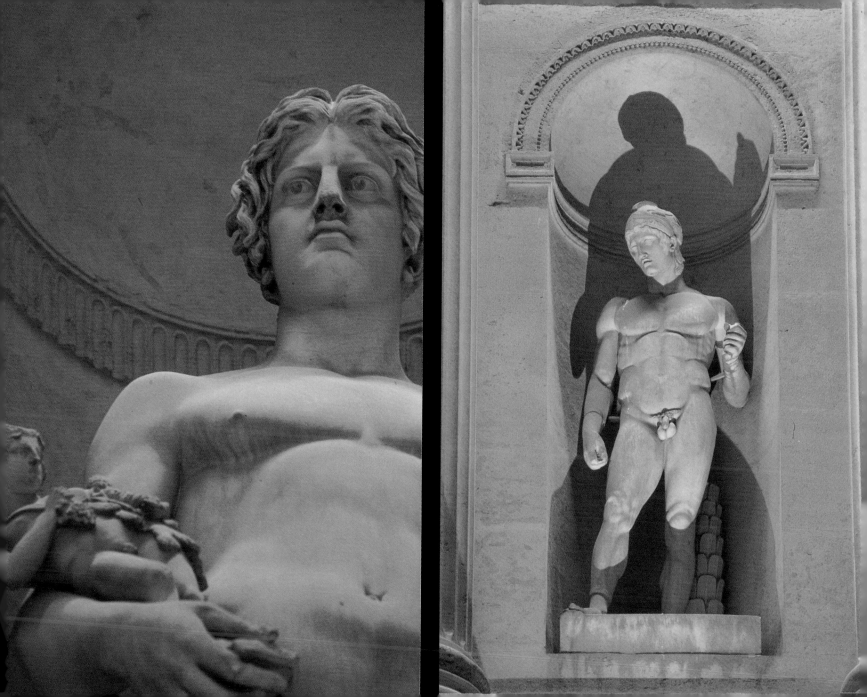

Combining

Guy Nicot

Guy Nicot is Chief Architect of Historic Monuments in France and curator of the Louvre Museum and Tuileries Gardens. He helped design the lighting for the two Louvre courtyards.

Stone and Light

The Louvre as we know it today is a stunning example of French architecture. Over the course of centuries architects followed without copying each other. All of them respected the Renaissance spirit that guided the great Pierre Lescot, the architect chosen by François I (1494-1547) to expand and modernize the medieval Louvre. The two courtyards' lighting had to respect the sites' harmony and take account of their special history.

Architecture is the art of ordering volumes. It is also the genius of bringing stone and light into harmony with one another. Daylight strikes and is reflected by facades. Windows let it into rooms. Their orientation has been of paramount importance since architecture began.

During the Middle Ages, walls were thick and windows few. Narrow slits were the only openings that let light into the building. Rain streamed down the walls' facing, which the overhanging roof barely protected.

During the Renaissance, cornices were built at each story to channel rainwater. They became a common architectural feature—and made it possible to create rows of sculpture. Facades opened up new possibilities for architectural balance and decoration. As a result, the very spirit of buildings changed.

The Renaissance left its mark on the cour Carrée. As kings succeeded one another on the throne of France, architects respected the original rhythm established by Pierre Lescot.

24-25

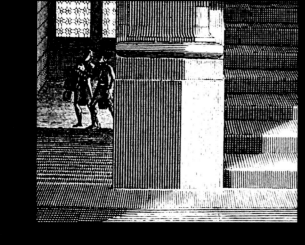

wing, which is a masterpiece of the Renaissance spirit. For three centuries this wing would remain a touchstone in the history of the Louvre. Each of the east facade's three stories has its own character. The three forewings provide the whole with a horizontal rhythm graced with magnificent sculptures. Lescot also innovated by designing the first broken pitched roof in France.

In 1624 Louis XIII commissioned Jacques Lemercier to carry on the Bourbon dream of a "Great Design" first envisioned by Henry IV. Cardinal Richelieu diligently oversaw the project. The kings were spending an increasing amount of their time in the Paris palace, which had to embody and represent the royal authority restored by Henry IV after thirty-six years of war. The "Great Design" consisted of quadrupling the size of the Old Louvre and rebuilding the space separating the two palaces.

After winning a competition Lemercier was chosen to extend the west wing northward. In 1664, at the beginning of the reign of Louis XIV, Le Vau, chief architect at Versailles, completed the inner facades of the cour Carrée. The outer facades, including Perrault's Colonnade to the east, were completed in 1670.

The different architects respected the unity established by Lescot and carried on by Lemercier. Sculpture gradually became less ornate in order to keep the whole from being weighed down by an ostentatious display of luxury. Each building stage was subtly distinct. The architecture's main lines provided the overall composition with perfect harmony.

26-27

The cour Carrée reflects changing daylight throughout the cycle of day and night. Light strikes each facade in turn as the sun continues its course across the sky, enhancing the projecting architectural elements and revealing the sculptures' depth.

" Recreating the subtlety of natural daylight was essential "

Recreating the subtlety of natural daylight and working with the lights' distribution, color and intensity were essential for illuminating the building at night. The first option consisted in recreating sunlight that looks as natural as possible by diffusing light from above. Low-angle lighting would have reversed the architectural effects and taken up room on the courtyard's floor.

A system that would not mar the facades with blinding spotlights had to be found. The idea of using the architecture's main lines, the cornices, to diffuse light was chosen.

turned out to be nearly ideal. The xenon lamps diffuse a warm tone similar to the color of the stone, contributing to the project's success. The intensity is adjusted depending on the delicacy of Jean Goujon's sculptures, revealing their outstanding beauty.

One of the greatest challenges lay in lighting the passageway from the cour Carrée to the cour Napoléon. The cour Napoléon opens out on to the Tuileries gardens, which lie in the Champs-Elysées axis designed by Le Nôtre. The special characteristics of the cour Napoléon made it necessary to adopt a different approach from the one used in lighting the cour Carrée.

In the mid-nineteenth century Napoleon III launched the Louvre's second "Grand Design". He was still president of the Second Republic in 1849 when Victor Hugo, representing Paris in the National Assembly, expressed his opinion on the project: "Creating a sort of metropolitan edifice of intellligence, establishing the rule of thought where kings once reigned... replacing the

28-29

greatness of the throne with the brightness of genius...
is a beautiful and high-minded idea."

As it turned out, the planned expansion was completed
under the Second Empire rather than the short-lived Second
Republic. Visconti and Lefuel designed the cour Napoléon,
which carries on the architectural mood of the cour Carrée.
The two courtyards are very different from one another, so
a group of details was designed to establish a sense of continuity between them. The rhythm of seven pavilions thus
recalls that of the pavilions in the cour Carrée. The arcades
open out on to a real gallery towards the gardens, clearing
the terraces. Allegories surrounding the bull's-eye windows
are all that remain of the ancient-style bas-reliefs. The sculpture, the groups by Barye, the eighty-six Illustrious Men and
their matching Geniuses on the upper balustrade were new
elements. Lastly, the destruction of the Tuileries chateau
opened the Louvre up to the gardens, freezing it
in a particular moment in its history. All of these unique
characteristics required special lighting.

illuminating the cour Napoléon fits in with a historical and visual continuity that ushers visitors from the strong light of the cour Carrée to the dark atmosphere of the gardens. The bright atmosphere creates a transition and smoothly leads to the dusky gardens where the triumphal Carrousel arch and the Tuileries statues stand out.

The lighting in the cour Napoléon is organized around the bright pyramid. Lampposts evenly aligned around the glass mass heighten the effect of this light source. The covered gallery is illuminated with safety lighting that can be dimmed or brightened depending on the events taking place at the museum.

An occasional similarity to the lighting in the cour Carrée underscores the pavilions' sculptural richness. A few low-angle lights heighten this effect. Spotlights on the terraces illuminate the plain facades. The space is flooded with so much light that the Illustrious Men sculptural group does not have to be illuminated by harsh spotlights.

30-31

The lighting of the Louvre facades on the banks of the Seine and the rue de Rivoli will complete the project. A recent cleaning has restored these facades' cream-colored tones, so the lighting must be of limited intensity. Special lighting will be designed for Perrault's Colonnade because of its unique architecture and its relationship to the cour Carrée.

The light of the Louvre shines forth from the central harmony of the cour Carrée. When the project is finished it will be in complete harmony with history as well as with our feelings.

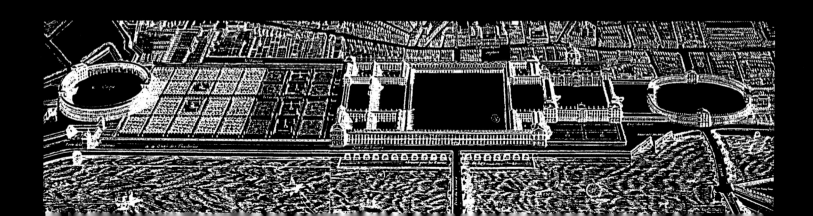

From Chinese
to

Geneviève Bresc

**Geneviève Bresc is curator of the Louvre sculpture
department as well as a historian of the museum.**

Lanterns
Everyday Lighting

The Louvre's exceptional status as both ceremonial palace and palace of the nation has always made it an important site of official festivals and celebrations. The cour Carrée and, later, the cour Napoléon have been spectacularly lit for these events. Second Empire city planners and architects equipped the courtyards with an early urban lighting system. The Grand Louvre has inherited and revitalized this two-fold tradition.

Lighting the Louvre at night is not a late twentieth-century idea. As early as the 1700s, when the Louvre was a ceremonial palace, the building was extravagantly lit for lavish royal celebrations. The Seine facade was entirely decorated with lighted garlands and the Grande Galerie ablaze with light from the inside. Small lights were hung in patterns on the stone facades and the balconies were laden with baskets of Chinese lanterns. The profusion of flickering flames must have been a spectacular sight in a city that was pitch black after nightfall.

After the French Revolution the Louvre became the palace of the nation. In 1793 it was officially designated a museum. The revolutionaries took up an old project already well under way during the reign of Louis XVI. The Louvre went from being a palace of royal festivals to one of national celebrations. From now on it was to host major events exalting the Revolution and, later, the Empire. For example, in 1801 the Louvre was the site of a festival in honor of the Products of Industry. This celebration was the forerunner of a long series of science and industry exhibitions. The event took place in the cour Carrée, which was illuminated with huge chandeliers and small lights installed on the cornices.

The cour Carrée was going to remain the magical site of great national celebrations throughout the nineteenth and twentieth centuries. In 1973 André Malraux's funeral was held in the courtyard, and in 1994 the banquet of French mayors took place there. In both cases the Louvre played a symbolic role as palace of the Nation.

" the cour Carrée was going to remain the magical site of great celebrations "

This status was established early in the Louvre's history, and it would be hard to find a building anywhere in the world that fulfills the same role. Henry IV had artists' accommodations set up in the Grand Gallery. The king's grandson, Louis XIV, followed his example and opened the palace to artists and their works. He had the distinguished academies, including the Académie française, and the Academy of Painting, move into the Louvre.

In the nineteenth century Napoleon III wanted to restore the Louvre's shining status as part of Baron Haussmann's plan to redesign Paris. Under the Republic the government had had the Old Louvre restored and the cour Carrée improved. In 1852, when Napoleon III ruled France with an iron grip after crushing the country's democratic institutions, he launched the massive cour Napoléon construction project. The two courtyards were equipped with a lighting system. In 1851 the cour Carrée was fitted out with small, round-based street lamps designed by the architect Duban. In 1857 the cour Napoléon was lit by large lamps crowning beautiful lampposts. The architect Hector Lefuel was so proud of them that he had Marville, one of the era's best photographers, take pictures of them. The closely spaced lampposts flooded the courtyard with bright light. I.M. Pei had them put back when the pyramid was built. The cour des Écuries has tall lamps crowning marble columns. Lastly

38-39

a row of street lamps runs along the entire rue de Rivoli facade. The passage Richelieu, which connects the city with the cour Napoléon, is also graced with tall lampposts. Of course these lights are electric, but the twelve-foot long lamp-lighter's rod is still stored in the museum's vault. Before 1860 there were few public lamps in Paris, and they were all gaslights.

The apartments of the emperor in the Tuileries and of the minister of State had huge, brightly shining chandeliers, but the museum was still dark after sundown, at least most of the time. For no privilege was more fashionable or more sought-after than a nighttime visit to the Louvre in the flickering light of enormous torches borne by footmen. Any present-day curator, not to mention firefighter, would break out into a cold sweat at the mere thought of these guided tours! Visiting officials and rulers enjoyed these torchlit moonlight strolls. At night Napoleon I used to gaze at the Vatican Laocoön, which his army had brought to Paris after plundering Italy. Later on visitors admired the Venus de

Milo in the dramatic torchlight. Artists and poets dreamed of a night visit, a rare privilege. It was one of the dying Alfred de Musset's last wishes, and he got it. We can picture, then, the very dark museum framed by a very bright setting during the second half of the nineteenth century.

Celebrations showcased the Louvre's exterior. The imperial regime staged receptions whose extravagant lighting was extended from the Tuileries gardens. The 1869 World's Fair made lavish use of this setting. This is when Paris earned its nickname "the city of light".

In 1936 the generous spirit of the Popular Front was in the air. The museum's director, Henri Verne, decided to illuminate the Louvre with electric lights at night. The ancient sculpture rooms were the first to be opened to the public after dark. Next came the other sculpture rooms and the archaeological department's new crypts. Keeping the museum open at night made attendance more democratic, since workers now had increased opportunities to view the collections. Lighting the facades after sundown became more necessary than ever. Proud of his achievement, Verne even published a little book entitled *Le Louvre la Nuit* to extol this modern advance.

The creation of the Grand Louvre marked a new step in the museum's history. The building attracts throngs of French and international strollers and visitors. The Louvre is a focal point of artistic, cultural and commercial activities that continue after dark. Twice a week the museum is open in the evening. Crowds as well as the goal of giving the building a contemporary luster required a type of lighting that would do more than guide and protect. It had to become an integral part of enhancing the site's beauty.

"Paris earned its nickname 'the city of light'"

The idea was not new. An attempt to light the cour Carrée was made during André Malraux's tenure as French minister of culture in the sixties. Spotlights perched atop lampposts cast such a harsh glare on the facades that the project was considered a failure and dropped.

The present system comes as close as possible to natural daylight and respects the courtyards' original harmony. In its own way the lighting sculpts the Louvre's facades. It brings out contrasts between light and dark instead of eliminating shadows with harsh, flattening spotlights. It sets off the transition between buildings and makes volumes stand out. It allows visitors to have their own personal view of the architecture.

One must imagine the dim glimmer that long flickered on the Louvre's facades to appreciate how contemporary the present lighting is. Flaming torches and gaslights once cast theatrical, moving shadows. In contrast, soft, stable and motionless electric light is as smooth and timeless as the stone with which it seems to be engaging in dialogue.

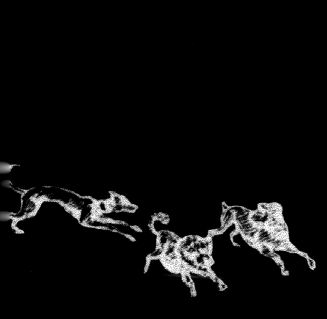

44-45

In the Shelt

Arlette Farge

Arlette Farge is a historian who writes about daily life in the eighteenth-century city. Her sources include contemporary archives, diaries and police reports.

ering

Shadow of Paris

In eighteenth-century Paris light was rare, frail and flickering at night. After sundown only the daring ventured out among shadows and phantoms. Several thousand lanterns swayed in the streets. These lamps, beloved and hated at the same time, both guided Parisians and kept them under surveillance. Darkness protected lovers, thieves and doctors—and surrounded the flames reflected in the eyes of the figures painted by the artist Georges de La Tour.

Nighttime Paris was unsafe, dark and watchful. At dusk the city and its walls flickered with reddish, glowing light. Candles glimmered inside windows while outside lanterns set up in star patterns blazed above the pavement. When night fell in winter, laborers left their workshops. Builders with plaster on their soles left their construction sites. Their steps could be heard, but their identities could not be made out in the darkness. All that could be discerned were the whitish footprints left by their shoes, pale tracks that lightly lit the ground, guiding the way to quarters outside the city walls better than any false friend.

Lanterns swayed back and forth on the middle of ropes hung between buildings. The city had been lit since 1667, and the torch holders still served their purpose. They led passersby to streets with lampposts.

Eyes searched the darkness for the familiar way, the streetwalker, the waiting carriage, the friend and the neighbor. The police installed 2,700 lanterns at the beginning of the eighteenth century, 5,000 towards the middle and another 8,000 shortly before the French Revolution broke out in 1789. Lighting was rare, all the more so when the moon was full and the lamps were left unlit to save money. Parisians had to patiently wait for the bright, silvery disk to rise before the streets gleamed with light.

" when the moon was full the lamps were left unlit to save money "

The enemy was gusting winds, which shook and blew out the lanterns. When that happened hurrying passersby kept their eyes on the next one, reestablishing the chain of light that usually led them onward. The dark landmarks of Paris were far from reassuring and even offered some odd spectacles. In the eighteenth century the Louvre's majestic colonnade was partly hidden by slipshod used clothes stalls where masons and laborers came to buy garments already parasols were folded up at night they looked like motionless giants in the darkness. At first sight the unaware passerby retreated in the darkness; he could not have guessed what those phantoms were." In addition the still-unfinished Louvre was covered with scaffolding. At night their shadows seemed to softly groan and punch holes in the sky.

Workers were clearing the cemetery of the Innocents in the heart of the tired, feverish city, unearthing buried corpses by torchlight. Further on, barely hidden, crouching doctors secretly dragged bodies out of common graves to study their anatomy by candlelight. Tombs and gloomy flames gave rise to a pathetic atmosphere that later was to inspire poets. For now, everyone still believed that restless souls were turning over under the ground.

Parisians enjoyed seeing but not being seen. They hated lamps as much as they appreciated them. Lanterns kept the city's residents under a watchful glare, shedding light on dark corners where lovers or thieves would rather remain

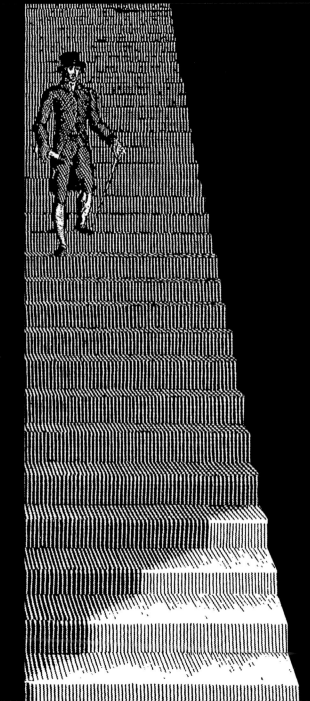

invisible. Light helped the police monitor the population. As in the days when craftsmen engraved street names on buildings, the lanterns could be installed only at night to avoid stirring the ire of passersby.

Light protected and threatened at the same time. Parisians could hear the crystalline laughter of passersby and the crash of glass being shattered by fellow residents trying to put out the lamps. This childish antic was a gesture of anarchy and freedom for those who dared to dream. The chain of lanterns always emerged the victor, for light rhymed with life in the eighteenth-century city.

Paris revolutionaries sang of hanging aristocrats from the lampposts. The insurrectionary crowd wanted to put things to right their own way. The angry mob considered lanterns the aristocrats' tools in keeping the people under surveillance. What better symbolism than to use one to get rid of the other?

Sundown was not the only thing that darkened Paris. Thick fog often crept into the city along its walls. Torches were of no use in the cold air. In 1765 the fog was so dense someone had the far-fetched idea of renting out blind people from the eye hospital to walk residents through the streets. For five louis a day, Parisians could let a blind person guide them by hanging on to his or her robe. When day was more like night, the sightless surefootedly led their clients through all the city's nooks and crannies in a strange procession.

If Parisians wanted to find bright light they had to go to the churches, especially Saint Sulpice, where God's host dazzled a crowd of admirers. L. S. Mercier wrote that "hearts melted with love" at the sight. Returning home afterwards was never a simple matter, especially since the city authorities had building doors locked at night. After eleven p.m. residents could not get into their own homes unless they owned one of the mansions in the Marais. Countless arguments constantly broke out over these lockouts. People returning home late had to run after the keepers of the keys and convince them to open the heavy

As a historian I have always pictured Paris at night as a dark lake dotted with flames, candles, flying sparks and burning brands carried down the Gobelins hills to the Bièvre river by washerwomen in the pre-dawn hours. In the early morning or late at night workers carrying lanterns scurried through the city streets. These shadowy figures wore faces as long as the day. On nights when kings and princesses staged festivals, fireworks and sparkling spinning wheels lit up the sky. The crowd gazed at the spectacle as if stars were really falling on a world that was always dark.

Fire was respected because it provided light and warmth, dreaded because, along with epidemics, it was one of the eighteenth century's worst plagues. In 1718 E. J. Barbier began his diary entry with an account of the terrible Petit Pont fire that destroyed all the houses lining the Seine. The eight-hour blaze was sparked by an innocent and pious gesture. A woman's son had drowned. To find his body she floated a small wooden bowl carrying a candle and a loaf of Saint Nicholas bread on the river. The mother made the offering to Saint Nicholas in the hopes that he would ease her grief. The bowl floated smoothly along for a while before bumping into a hay-laden barge moored at the quai de la Tournelle. The candle turned the dry cargo into one huge torch.

The city was vulnerable. At night thousands of candles made brass softly glimmer, reddened young maidens' cheeks, shined on the wan skin of corpses and enabled learned men to read. The painter La Tour knew that the candle's flame and the child's hand protecting it were the essence of beauty. The flame represented warmth as well as ephemeralness, for it could vanish in a flow of

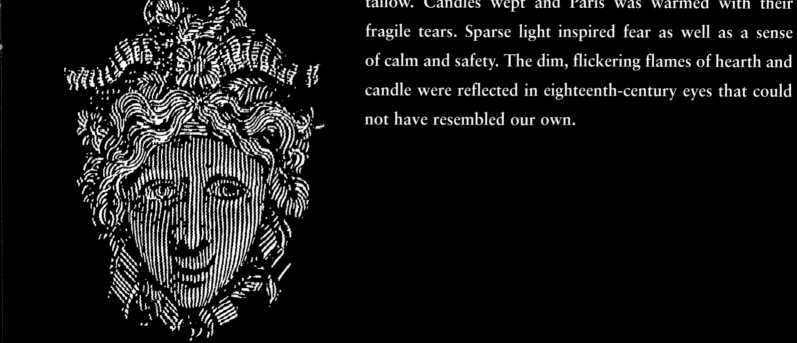

tallow. Candles wept and Paris was warmed with their fragile tears. Sparse light inspired fear as well as a sense of calm and safety. The dim, flickering flames of hearth and candle were reflected in eighteenth-century eyes that could not have resembled our own.

Changing

is

Cinematographer Henri Alekan has shot more than 100 films, from Jean Cocteau's and René Clément's *La Belle et La Bête* to Wim Wenders' *Wings of Desire*. He has also written a book that is now a reference, *Des lumières et des ombres*, and designed the lighting for many monuments.

Light
Changing Life

The lighting of the Louvre is modeled after natural sunlight and respects the visitor's viewpoint. In this regard it is completely different from cinema or theater lighting, which dramatizes in order to arouse feelings. Cinematographers are always amazed at the magic of light, and dream of the mood that arbitrary, subjective motion picture or theater lighting would give a huge urban setting.

For a long time the Louvre was like a vast shadow in the middle of Paris. It was one of the darkest places in the city of light.

Twenty years ago I designed the lighting for a television show filmed inside the museum. The stage had been set up on the Winged Victory staircase. We had to shoot night scenes partly lit by the lights outside. The technicians wanted my lighting to be as soft as possible. They said their cameras were powerful enough to capture the light from outside. Highly doubtful, I remember saying, "But the Louvre courtyards are the most dimly lit places in Paris!" I turned out to be right, and in twenty-four hours we set up a high-powered, very bright lighting system that gave the usually imposing, gloomy Louvre a short-lived festive air.

This incident came to mind during a recent walk at the Louvre. The new lighting creates a particularly powerful effect in the cour Carrée.

Like all landmarks in French cities, the Louvre was not designed with the idea of night illumination in mind. It was

built to be seen in sunlight. Now, it is impossible to reproduce sunlight because it comes from above and changes from one moment to the next. Intensity and quality vary substantially from dawn to dusk, so each moment of the day arouses a particular feeling. This light has always dazzled me. I think it has a tremendous impact on our thoughts and acts, and it links us to the cosmos.

I believe the architects who designed French monuments could not have imagined their achievements being seen in anything other than daylight. Artificial light completely changes our perceptions. It is a mental construction, the outcome of an aesthetic decision and the result of a desire to bring about a particular emotion or mood.

The Louvre's lighting is intended to resemble natural daylight as much as possible. Of course sunshine cannot be imitated, but the designers decided to respect the play of light and shadow that daylight casts on architecture. The use of low-angle lighting, which is the norm with historic landmarks and in motion pictures, was ruled out,

This kind of lighting creates an unusual or even eerie mood because it reverses the natural play of shadow and light.

If low-angle lighting alone had been used to illuminate the Louvre, the wrong effect would have been achieved. It would have given the architecture the opposite meaning of what had been intended. The warm, uniform lighting that has been chosen quietly underscores the reliefs. In a way it is objective because it does not seek to stir a particular emotion and respects each visitor's viewpoint. It does not impose a perspective and lets strollers look at whatever they want to.

It is very unusual to see lighting like this in the movies. The only example I have ever come across is in William Wyler's *Roman Holiday*. I had to light a scene with the Castel Sant'Angelo and the banks of the Tiber in the background. I opted for bright, cheerful lighting that would match the image of the movie, which is about a young princess, played by Audrey Hepburn, who, for the first time, falls in love in Rome with an older man, played by Gregory Peck

62-63

If I had been asked to light the Louvre for a motion picture—the site would make a magnificent set—I would have tried to immerse the audience in a thoroughly artificial atmosphere, an unreal world where anything is possible. I would have modulated the light more to achieve that goal, but motion picture lighting has neither the same purpose nor the same limitations as permanent lighting for a public site. In the movies, light helps the director reinvent reality, express his or her subjective vision and trigger emotions. The cinematographer cheats by installing lighting equipment wherever he wants to depending on the effect sought in a given scene. Everything depends on the character of the film or the sequence. The light may be dramatic. In that case sharp contrasts and dark shadows would be in order to stress the tension. If a light comedy is being filmed, the lighting would be softer, more golden and more psychological. In any case, the goal is always to create a certain mood with light.

cinematographer's eyes. I dream of cities where the streets and landmarks would be lit like a movie set. Light is like music: it could give our walks rhythm and variations. Why not imagine a city where artificial light would compose a palette of feelings at night? For instance, I would use theater spotlights to illuminate facades, stressing some parts while others would remain dark. I would alternate serene, simple, poetic and melancholic moonlight with lively, complex, strong and warm artificial light.

I would like to light streets, buildings and bridges. When we finished *Wings of Desire* Wim Wenders poetically defined his profession by saying, "If we improve the images of the world, we improve life." I would put my own personal twist on this statement by saying, if we improve the lights of the city, we improve life.

64-65

Table of illustrations

P. 2: *Abundance* or *Nature*, by Jean Goujon, 1548-1553. Cour Carrée, Lescot wing, 1st left forewing. © La Photothèque EDF/Claude Pauquet.

P. 5: © Musy.

P. 6-7: cour Napoléon, general view. Hector Lefuel, architect, 1854-1857. © La Photothèque EDF/Claude Pauquet.

P. 8-9: *Caryatids*, by Gilles Guérin and Philippe de Buyster, after models by Jacques Sarazin, 1639-1642. Cour Carrée, pavillon de l'Horloge. © La Photothèque EDF/Claude Pauquet.

P. 10-11: cour Carrée, left, Lescot (or Henry II) wing; center, pavillon de l'Horloge; right, the Lemercier (or Henry IV) wing. © La Photothèque EDF/Claude Pauquet.

P. 12: left, copy of a *Roman Empress* from the Vatican Museum. Cour Carrée, Lemercier wing, left forewing; right, *Aphrodite*, by Clère, 1859. Cour Carrée, south facade. © La Photothèque EDF/Claude Pauquet.

P. 13: left, *Euripyle*, by Iselin, 1860. Cour Carrée, west facade; right, copy of the *Borghese Mars* (MA 866) from the Louvre Museum. Cour Carrée, Lescot

wing, 1st right forewing. © La Photothèque EDF/Claude Pauquet.

P. 14-15: left, *Minerva Rewarding the Fine Arts and the Sciences*, by Jacques-Philippe Le Sueur, 1811. Cour Carrée, pavillon des Arts, pediment. © La Photothèque EDF/Claude Pauquet.

P. 16-17: *Caryatids*, by Gilles Guérin and Philippe de Buyster after models by Jacques Sarazin, 1639-1642. Cour Carrée, pavillon de l'Horloge. © La Photothèque EDF/Claude Pauquet.

P. 18-19: left to right, *Moses, Isis, Manco-Capac, Numa*, by Jean-Guillaume Moitte, 1808-1810. Cour Carrée, Lemercier wing, 1st right forewing. © La Photothèque EDF/Claude Pauquet.

P. 22: *The Law*, by Jean-Guillaume Moitte, 1808-1810. Cour Carrée, Lemercier wing, left forewing.© La Photothèque EDF/Claude Pauquet.

Pp. 25 and 29: © Musy.

P. 31: *The Great Design*, project for the Louvre palace. Engraving by Houdin, 1661. Paris, Musée Carnavalet. © Giraudon.

P. 34: *Henry II as the God Mars and Captive Viewed from the*

Front, by Jean Goujon, 1548-1543. Cour Carrée, Lescot wing, 2nd central forewing, attic. © La Photothèque EDF/Claude Pauquet.

Pp. 38, 39 and 43: © Giraudon.

P. 46: *Angel Bearing the Coat of Arms of France* (replaced by a rooster), by Guillaume II Coustou, 1757-1759. Cour Carrée, east wing, central pavilion. © La Photothèque EDF/Claude Pauquet.

Pp. 51 and 55: © Musy.

P. 58: after a model by Jacques Sarazin, 1639-1642. Cour Carrée, Lemercier wing, 2nd central forewing .© La Photothèque EDF/Claude Pauquet.

Pp. 61 and 65: © Musy.

Pp. 66-67: cour Carrée, general view of the Lescot and Marengo wings. © La Photothèque EDF/Claude Pauquet.

P. 68: left, *Christian Art*, by Emile Chatrousse, 1860; right, *Sappho with Her Lyre*, by Pierre Travaux, 1857. Cour Carrée, east part of the north wing, ground floor. © La Photothèque EDF/Claude Pauquet.

P. 69: left, copy of the *Faun Playing a Flute* (MA 594) from the Louvre Museum. Cour Carrée, pavillon des Arts, 1st storey, right, 3rd left forewing; right, copy of *Euterpe* (MA 414)

from the Louvre Museum. Cour Carrée, aile des Arts, 1st storey, right, 2nd right forewing. © La Photothèque EDF/Claude Pauquet.

P. 70: Decoration of the clock by Lemercier after models by Jacques Sarazin. Cour Carrée, pavillon de l'Horloge. © La Photothèque EDF/Claude Pauquet.

P. 71: *Glory and Peace*, by Etienne-Jules Ramey, 1825-1827. Cour Carrée, north wing, east section, left bull's-eye. © La Photothèque EDF/Claude Pauquet.

P. 72: *The Genius of France Encouraging the Arts*, by Etienne-Jules Ramey, around 1810. Cour Carrée, north wing, pediment. © La Photothèque EDF/Claude Pauquet.

P. 73: *Angel Bearing the Coat of Arms of France* (replaced by a rooster), by Guillaume II Coustou, 1757-1759. Cour Carrée, central pavilion of the east wing. © La Photothèque EDF/Claude Pauquet.

P. 74: *Victory*, by Philippe-Laurent Roland, 1808-1810. Cour Carrée, 2nd central forewing, pediment. © La Photothèque EDF/Jean-Marc Charles.

P. 75: left, *Heroic Poetry*, by Antoine-Denis Chaudet, 1808-

1810, right, *Science*, by Jean Goujon, 1548-1553. Cour Carrée, Lescot wing, 3rd right forewing, attic. © La Photothèque EDF/Claude Pauquet.

Pp. 76-77: left, copy of the *Aphrodite Anadyomen* (n° 667) from the Vatican Museum. Cour Carrée, pavillon des Arts, 1st storey, right, 2nd right forewing; right, *The Illustrious Men*, cour Napoléon, Mollien wing. © La Photothèque EDF/Claude Pauquet.

Pp. 78-79: cour Napoléon, general view. © La Photothèque EDF/Claude Pauquet.

P. 80: cour Carrée, pavillon de l'Horloge.

Pp. II-III: © Guy Nicot/D.R.

Printed May 1995 by Alba Graphic in Montreuil.

Lighting the Louvre: An Inside Account

Rarely has so much attention been paid to lighting a monument. Electricité de France and its partners—researchers and manufacturers—have rediscovered the science of lighting to illuminate the facades of the cour Carrée and the cour Napoléon, boldly setting off the achievements of the architects and sculptors of the kings of France. They have used state-of-the-art technology to show the courtyards' classical sculpture off to its best advantage. This is the story of an artistic and technological adventure.

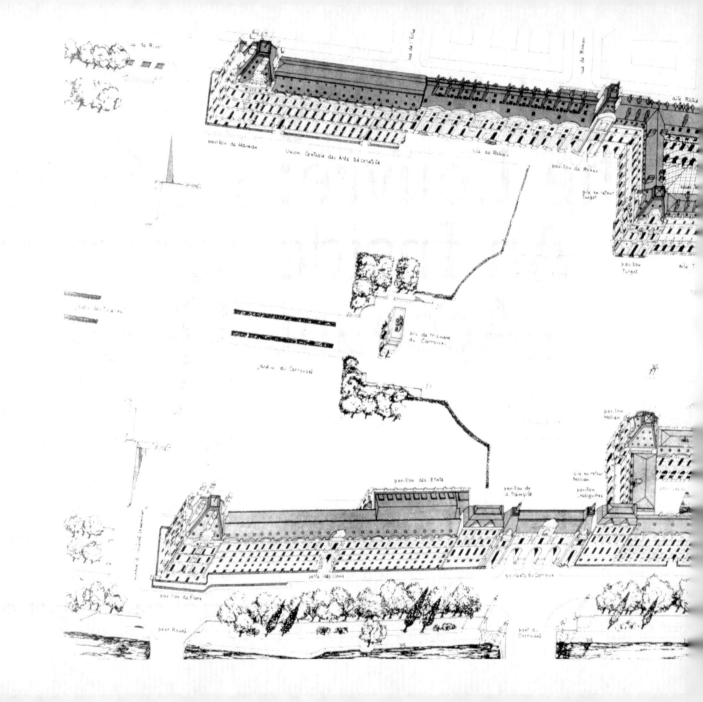

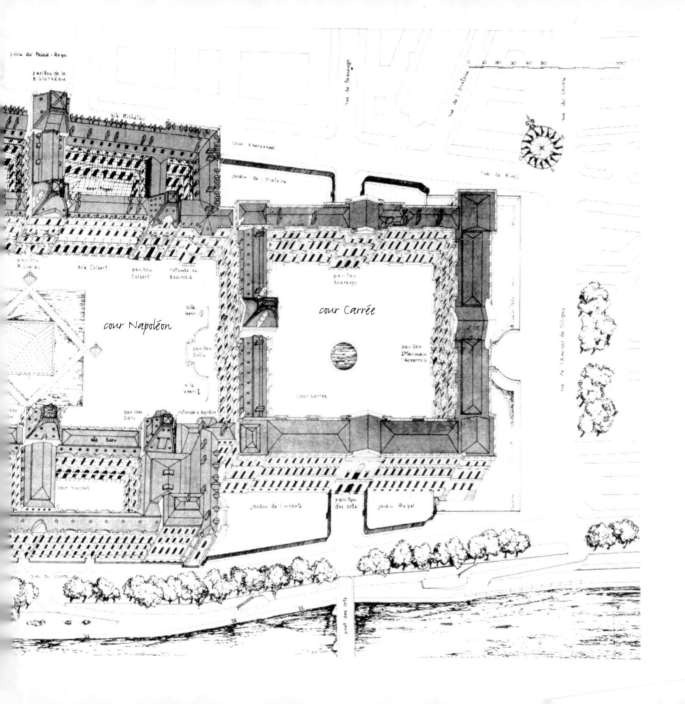

place du Palais-Royal

pavillon de la
Bibliothèque

aile Richelieu

rue de Marengo

rue de l'Oratoire

rue du Louvre

0 10 20 30 40 50   100

cour Lefuel

jardin de l'Oratoire

rue de Rivoli

pavillon
Richelieu

aile Colbert   pavillon   rotonde de
Colbert   Beauvais

cour Napoléon

pavillon
Marengo

cour Carrée

aile
Henri IV

pavillon
Sully

aile
Henri II

pavillon
St Germain
l'Auxerrois

cour carrée

rue de l'Amiral de Coligny

pavillon
Daru   rotonde d'Apollon

aile Daru

cour Visconti

jardin de l'Infante

pavillon
des arts

jardin Raffet

quai du Louvre

pont des arts

The technological epic that culminated in lighting the Louvre began in 1991. It took over three years to match skills with tasks, coordinate cultural, historical and technical demands and find the best lighting harmonies. EDF's Public Lighting Department, the Research and Development Division and the CNRS (Centre National de Recherche Scientifique – National Science Research Center) pooled their skills and knowledge. Everything had to be invented from scratch. The main lighting options had to be tested and chosen, the specifications drawn up and the equipment developed and installed.

Light Playing on a Virtual Palace

When EDF suggested illuminating the Louvre courtyards to the museum's directors, a variety of lighting possibilities had to be imagined. Until then, lighting designers had based their work on more or less accurate real and virtual models. These models were based on architects' plans and made it possible to visualize the lighting project, but only approximately. The results were sometimes full of surprises.

At the Louvre, for the first time a completed monumental project looked exactly the way it did in the design stage. Computer tools were specially developed for the project. The variety of possible night lightings designed looked almost completely realistic.

The Louvre courtyards were "virtualized". The facades were modeled on the basis of existing plans or hand-drawn elevations. For some of the Sully pavilion's details, EDF's Research and Development Division and the Mensi Company used the same process they did to obtain accurate elevations of certain parts inside nuclear power plants and the modeling of the Pont Neuf. A laser beam scanned the august facades, optically reading the smallest details down to less than a millimeter. The reliefs were recorded, creating an extraordinarily faithful digital replica of the actual surface. The digital data were then converted

Laser beams took an optical reading of the most complex forms.

soisic sensor

into color geometric shapes such as flat surfaces and cylinders. That is how the Louvre courtyards were dematerialized without losing the least amount of detail.

A computer program called Phostère was specially designed to process the laser images and simulate the lighting. The software is based on complex mathematical equations and light propa-gation principles. This program requires such powerful computers that it could not be developed until the late 1980s. EDF joined forces with the CNRS Computer Research Center in Nancy to develop Phostère. The software takes into consideration all the light sources' characteristics, such as color, intensity, inclination and adjustment. Phostère integrates materials-related variables, for stone does not catch light the same way zinc or marble does. Last but not least, the software applies features and variables to three-dimensional pictures. The light sources' positioning and special features create the same effect as in the real world.

The lighting designer can work on it until he or she is satisfied.

Combining laser imagery with Phostère allowed technicians to model various lighting possibilities on the computer. They were tested, displayed in trials on the buildings themselves and finally chosen.

Phostère, a program specially developed to simulate the different lighting possibilities.

An inventory of the
different types of pavilions
was taken. This is the
Turgot pavilion in the cour
Napoléon.

The Artist's Trompe l'œil

The choice that was to guide the lighting designers was clear from the outset. The lighting had to be incremental, increasing in intensity from dusk to the middle of the night. It also had to be zenithal, illuminating the surfaces directly from above. This was an innovative decision, since most monuments are lit at a low angle from the bottom up.

Zenithal lighting was chosen to respect the work of the architects and sculptors who designed and decorated the Louvre's cour Carrée. These artists had the sun's natural light in mind when they worked. Originally, they laid out the masses and proportions to interact with soft, variable, overhead sunlight. The goal of taming sunlight had led the sculptors

xenon lamps

High- and low-angle
lighting for the
caryatids.

Dichroic spotlights.

to carve the stone into trompes l'œil. Jean Goujon had calculated the proportions of the statues he sculpted in the cour Carrée so that they would look life-sized at noon. Low-angle lighting would have destroyed this effect, making the figures appear even longer than they already do.

The square-shaped, perfectly uniform cour Carrée is an architectural masterpiece. High-angle lighting was chosen for all the facades to respect the courtyard's perfection and to standardize shadows. Halogen spotlights illuminate the slate roof from the traditional low angle.

A combination of low- and high-angle lighting was chosen for some of the architectural elements, including the Sully pavilion clock, the caryatids and the bas-reliefs. This solution combines dichroic spotlights and xenon runway lights.

The cour Napoléon raised another set of problems for the lighting designers. This courtyard opens out on to the Tuileries gardens. The architecture is not as rich as in the cour Carrée, so it required

The Sully pavilion. Zenithal lighting is employed, except for the low-angle halogen lamps used for the roofs and back-up lights to underscore some details.

The cour Napoléon. Lighting of the terraced facades.

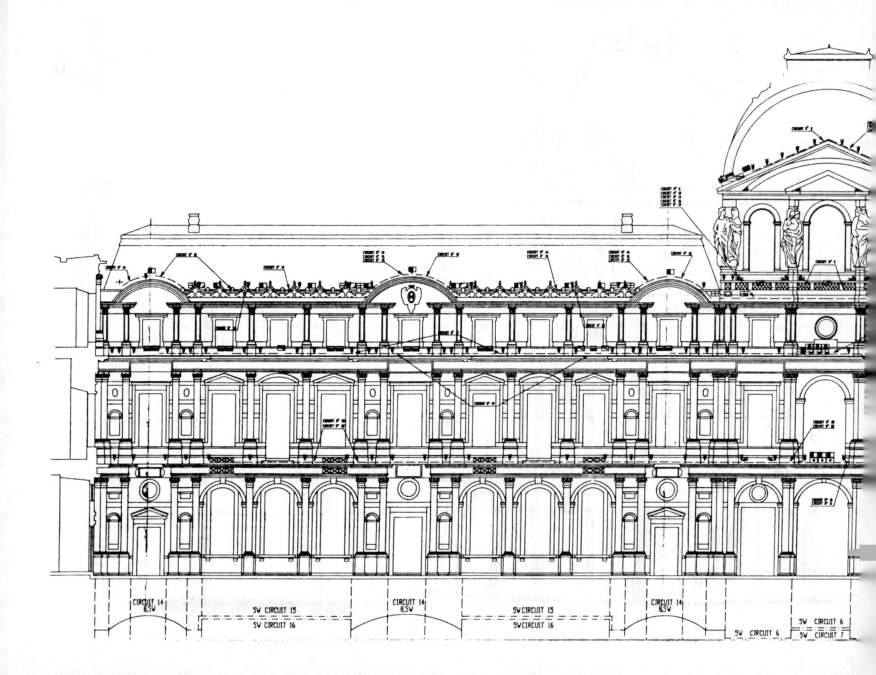

CIRCUIT 14
8,5V

5V CIRCUIT 15

5V CIRCUIT 16

CIRCUIT 14
8,5V

5V CIRCUIT 15

5V CIRCUIT 16

CIRCUIT 14
8,5V

5V CIRCUIT 6

5V CIRCUIT 6

5V CIRCUIT 6

5V CIRCUIT 7

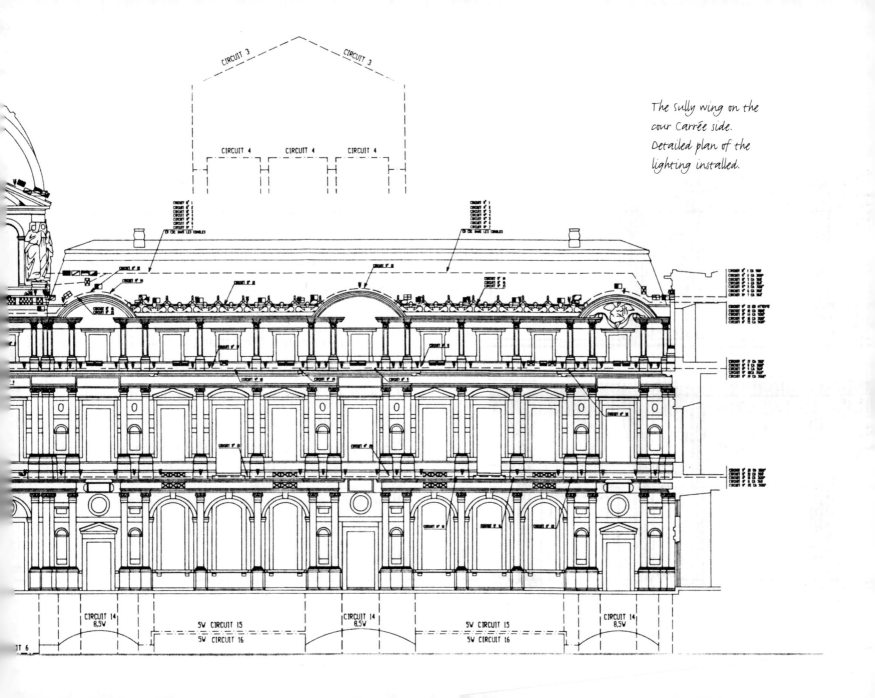

The Sully wing on the
cour Carrée side.
Detailed plan of the
lighting installed.

CIRCUIT 3   CIRCUIT 3

CIRCUIT 4   CIRCUIT 4   CIRCUIT 4

CIRCUIT 14   5W CIRCUIT 15   CIRCUIT 14   5W CIRCUIT 15   CIRCUIT 14
8,5W   5W CIRCUIT 16   8,5W   5W CIRCUIT 16   8,5W

a somewhat less sophisticated approach. Yet this space had to be "readable" from far away along the Champs Elysées axis as well as from close-up by the visitors walking across it. It was also important to keep a uniform perception of the Louvre encompassing the Tuileries gardens and to equip the courtyard with night lighting essential for the safety of passersby. Last but not least, I.M. Pei's glass pyramid had to remain the site's focal point.

Bathed in the new lighting, the pyramid looks like a jewel in its setting. The lighting is basically low-angle, except for a few architectural details lit from above. It sets off the seven pavilions that are architecturally similar to those in the cour Carrée. The lighting provides visitors moving from one space to the other with a sense of continuity. Neutral lighting illuminates the facades connecting the pavilions. Cold lights underscore the roofs, making them visible from afar.

Technology Developed for an Idea

The computer images were convincing, the choices were made, but the technology lagged behind. Aesthetic decisions had to be translated into concrete form. The search was on for a light source whose color was as close as possible to daylight's and that could fit into a small, robust device. Such an object did not exist, or at least not yet. It just had to be invented.

The ideal lamp had to comply with all sorts of requirements. The spotlights had to be sturdy enough to withstand bad weather and pollution, but could not mar the facades in the daytime. The discreet yet rugged lights had to be capable of illuminating the facades as evenly as the sun without blinding passersby.

They had to be beautiful, effective and energy efficient. Lastly, since maintenance requires the use of a 60-meter elevator, they had to be designed for minimum upkeep.

Technicians gradually began fulfilling the conditions set down in the specifications. Then they started looking for suppliers willing to develop hitherto non-existent products.

New Devices

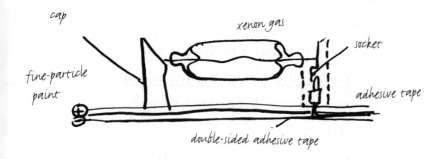

Xenon provides a warms tone. After an extensive search, the B-Light system was selected.

cap

xenon gas

socket

fine-particle paint

adhesive tape

double-sided adhesive tape

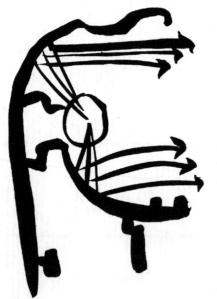

Cross-section of the aluminum ramps: many tests were carried out to calculate the ideal reflector's curves.

Incandescent lamps were chosen because they cast a golden light. However, the traditional light sources available on the market did not meet the Louvre's needs. Common light bulbs have a lifespan of approximately 1,000 hours, which is much too short. The lights illuminating Paris monuments last around 2,000 hours a year.

EDF specialists consulted a wide range of manufacturers before settling on a Swiss firm headed by Youri Agabekov, who invented the B-Light system and is famous for his illuminated interiors. One of this company's small, 1-cm., thick-filament xenon incandescent bulbs combined all the sought-after advantages. It has a warm color, an estimated lifespan of 10,000 hours—even after bad weather and pollution are taken into account—and low voltage, which helps prevent electric hazards. The bulb is energy efficient as well.

The right reflector still had to be found. It had to reflect the light by "frosting" the facades, which would send the rays back into space without blinding visitors strolling below. Engineers in the dark room of EDF's photometry lab tested sources and reflectors, using a gigantic adjustable mirror to measure how far the light radiated in space. The tests went on for several months, with a little curving here, a little flattening there. After numerous experiments and calculations, the ideal reflector was designed and made.

The new reflectors were fitted into aluminum ramps housing a series of parallel lamps. Designed for maintenance purposes to be easily dismantled, each ramp is 1.50 meters long, six centimeters wide and four centimeters high. The ramps house rows of twenty-five lamps behind a screen that prevents visitors from being blinded by the light.

The ramps were discreetly attached to the uneven cornices without altering the stone.

A Challenging Installation

Installing the ramps on the Louvre's venerable stone facade raised a new set of problems. The architectural elements, built by craftsmen and subjected to centuries of bad weather and air pollution, are not as sturdy as they look. The ramps had to be installed on cornices that turned out to be randomly uneven because of the thin layer of lead covering them as waterproofing. It was impossible to directly install the ramps without achieving somewhat chaotic results. Drilling holes in the facades would ruin the stone, so that option was ruled out.

The solution to this dilemma quickly became obvious. Tinplated brass legs were soldered on to the lead cornice. Their role is to support rails on which the ramps would be clipped. The finely adjusted aluminum rails made sure the lighting was perfectly straight. They also made it possible to easily install and remove each ramp part.

The first stage of the lighting of the cour Carrée was completed in October 1993. The Louvre's directors had specified that the project be finished by then to celebrate the museum's bicentennial and the inauguration of the Richelieu wing. It took less than six weeks to finish the task.

In July 1994 EDF finished installing the lighting for the cour Carrée. The company set up 1.8 kilometers of lighted ramps, 200 spotlights for the roof and the details and twenty kilometers of electric power cables. Seventy independent electric circuits dim or brighten the light depending on whether the

courtyard is being used for fashion shows, concerts, plays or other events.

In late October the facades of the cour Napoléon were equipped with a kilometer of linear lights, ninety spotlights for the roof and wings, ten kilometers of cables and seventy-two different circuits. The work site was open twenty-four hours a day and bustled with up to thirty technicians at the same time. In the fall of 1994 visitors to the Louvre courtyards were able to see the sculptural details at night for the first time in their long history. The operation came off without a hitch. Nothing was left to chance for the building that symbolizes Paris.